This book is dedicated to al
teaching their k
about the many joys o

MW01098263

LEGENDS OF BASEBALL

FROM AARON TO OZZIE

Written by Mike Suarez

Illustrated by Various Artists

On April 8, 1974, Hank Aaron hit his 715th home run to pass Babe Ruth's career total of 714, a record that stood for nearly 39 years. Aaron would retire with a total of 755. His claim to the most HR of all time stood for 33 years until Barry Bonds hit 756 in 2007 and retired with 762.

Photo: 1974 Atlanta Braves
Picture Pack (via tradingcarddb)
Illustration: Zulkifli Ramadhan
Hanan

Hammerin' Hank Aaron
knocked them out an awful lot

In addition to his illustrious hitting career, Babe Ruth also had 92 wins to go along with a 2.28 career ERA as a pitcher. An eventual trade from the Red Sox to the Yankees helped finance the play "My Lady Friends" (not "No, No, Nanette", as many believe). This trade, along with the success of Ruth and the Yankees that followed, would set "The Curse of the Bambino" into motion and haunt the Red Sox for decades to come. (more on "the curse" later)

Photo: George Grantham Bain
(via LOC)
Illustration: Zulkifli Ramadhan
Hanan

to pass the great Babe Ruth -
the first "Sultan of Swat."

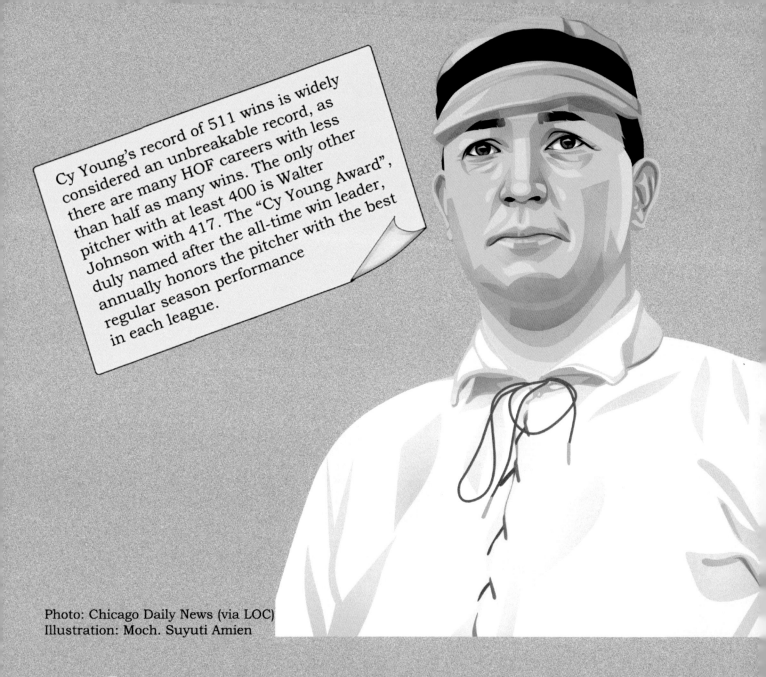

Cy Young's record of 511 wins is widely considered an unbreakable record, as there are many HOF careers with less than half as many wins. The only other pitcher with at least 400 is Walter Johnson with 417. The "Cy Young Award", duly named after the all-time win leader, annually honors the pitcher with the best regular season performance in each league.

Photo: Chicago Daily News (via LOC)
Illustration: Moch. Suyuti Amien

*C*y's the only guy with 500 wins on board.
Setting marks like that gets your name on an award.

Joltin' Joe DiMaggio recorded a hit in 56 consecutive games spanning from May 15, 1941 to July 17. That is just one of his many accomplishments to go along with 9 WS rings, 3 MVP's, 13 All-Star appearances and a .325 career batting average.

Photo: Prelinger Archives (via wikimedia)
Illustration: Zulkifli Ramadhan Hanan

Joe *Di* knows records too: a 56 game streak.
Guys would love to break it. Chances of that are bleak.

Ernie Banks is a member of the 500 HR club, with a career total of 512. Combined with his 14 All-Star berths, 2 MVP awards, and a Gold Glove, and it's easy to see why "Mr. Cub" was such a fan favorite on the north side of Chicago.

Photo: Bowman (via wikimedia)
Illustration: Suyudi Indrawijaya

"Ernie is Chicago's pride,"
Cub fans like to assert.

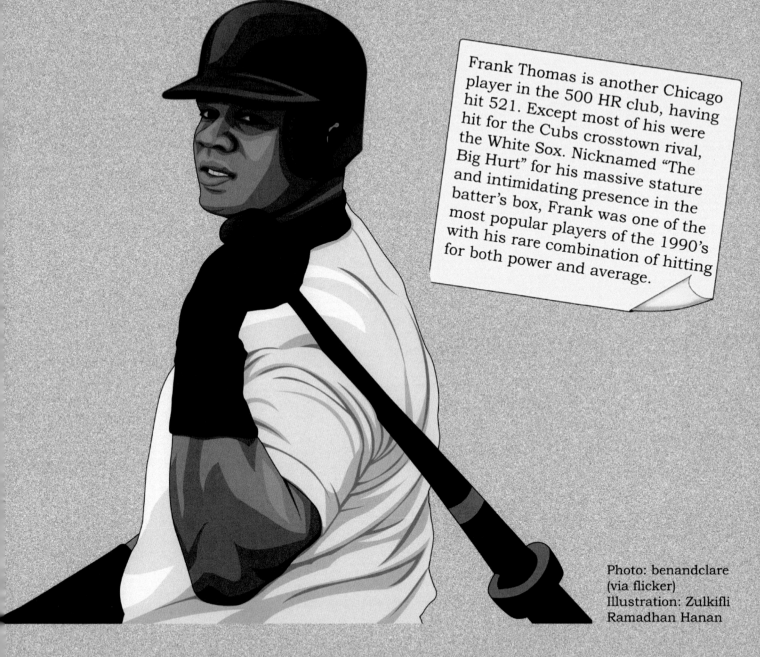

Frank Thomas is another Chicago player in the 500 HR club, having hit 521. Except most of his were hit for the Cubs crosstown rival, the White Sox. Nicknamed "The Big Hurt" for his massive stature and intimidating presence in the batter's box, Frank was one of the most popular players of the 1990's with his rare combination of hitting for both power and average.

Photo: benandclare (via flicker)
Illustration: Zulkifli Ramadhan Hanan

Say that on the South Side - Feel Frank Thomas' "Big Hurt."

GRIFFEY JR., OF

Speaking of popular players of the 90's, Ken Griffey Jr was the quintessential 5 tool player, amassing 630 HR, 184 SB, 8 seasons over .300, and 10 Gold Gloves. He dazzled fans with his HR robbing catches and pinpoint throws from center field. His skills and fun loving personality made him an instant fan favorite. Thus, his baseball cards were so coveted that they reinvigorated the baseball card market.

Photo: Best Cards (via tradingcarddb)
Illustration: Zulkifli Ramadhan Hanan

*G*riffey's loved by many fans.
His cards are very rare.

Besides being a historically great player, Honus Wagner's image is on what is widely considered the "Holy Grail" of baseball cards. Honus did not want his face on a card that was included in cigarette packs of various brands within the American Tobacco Company. So he had his card removed from production of the 1909-1911 T206 collection, but only after some 50-200 were printed. The rarity of the card makes it so desired that it recently sold for $3.12 million. If you want to own the version of the Honus Wagner card that was once famously owned by hockey legend, Wayne Gretzky, you'll have to talk to Diamondbacks owner Ken Kendrick, who bought that one for $2.8 million.

Photo: American Tobacco Company (via wikimedia)
Illustration: Moch. Suyuti Amien

Not as rare as *H*onus Wagner's card for millionaires.

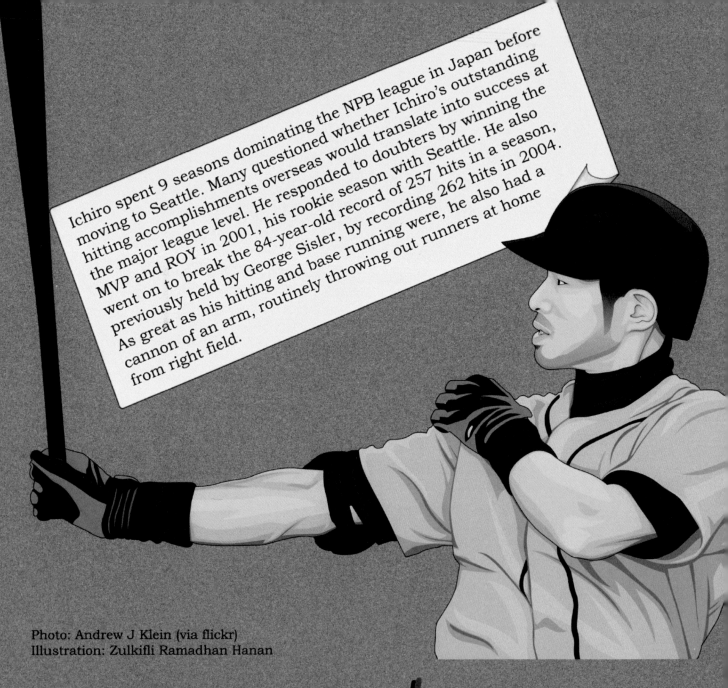

Ichiro spent 9 seasons dominating the NPB league in Japan before moving to Seattle. Many questioned whether Ichiro's outstanding hitting accomplishments overseas would translate into success at the major league level. He responded to doubters by winning the MVP and ROY in 2001, his rookie season with Seattle. He also went on to break the 84-year-old record of 257 hits in a season, previously held by George Sisler, by recording 262 hits in 2004. As great as his hitting and base running were, he also had a cannon of an arm, routinely throwing out runners at home from right field.

Photo: Andrew J Klein (via flickr)
Illustration: Zulkifli Ramadhan Hanan

Infield hits from Ichiro came from the left side.

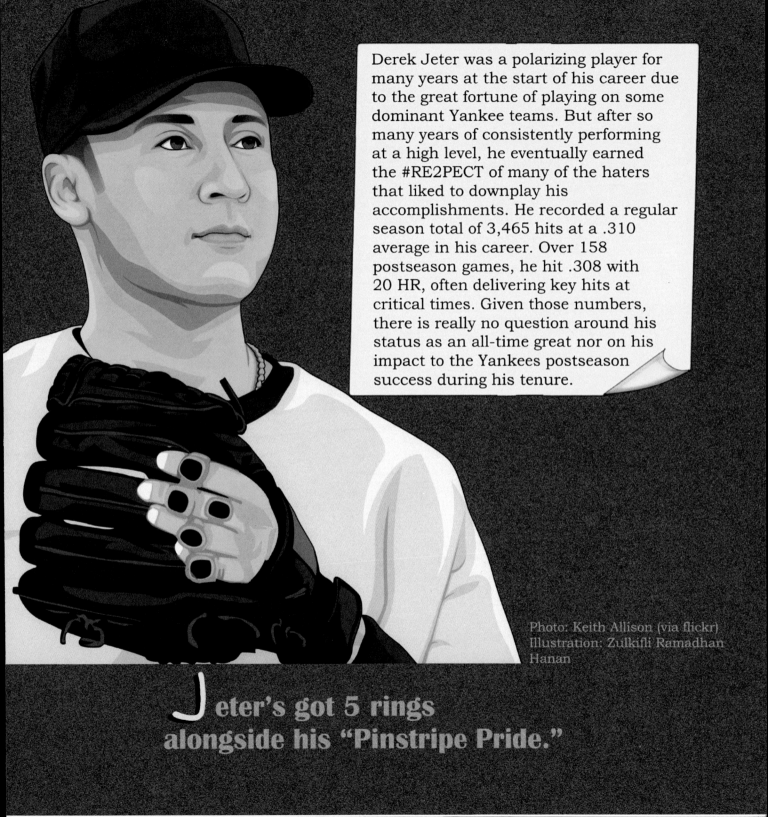

Derek Jeter was a polarizing player for many years at the start of his career due to the great fortune of playing on some dominant Yankee teams. But after so many years of consistently performing at a high level, he eventually earned the #RE2PECT of many of the haters that liked to downplay his accomplishments. He recorded a regular season total of 3,465 hits at a .310 average in his career. Over 158 postseason games, he hit .308 with 20 HR, often delivering key hits at critical times. Given those numbers, there is really no question around his status as an all-time great nor on his impact to the Yankees postseason success during his tenure.

Photo: Keith Allison (via flickr)
Illustration: Zulkifli Ramadhan Hanan

Jeter's got 5 rings alongside his "Pinstripe Pride."

Entering the 2019 season, Clayton Kershaw sports one of the lowest career ERA's of all time at 2.39. He's led the NL in ERA 5 times and finished below 2.00 in 3 different seasons. He's earned 7 All-Star appearances, 3 Cy Young awards, the Triple Crown, and the MVP (rare for a pitcher) all before he turned 30 years old.

Photo: Arturo Pardavila III (via flickr)
Illustration: Dharmawan Wicaksono

Kershaw's ERA is low, even for an ace.

50 SB would be enough to lead the league in many seasons. In 1974, one would have needed more than double that to surpass Lou Brock's 118 SB. Besides a couple of guys from 1887 that have more in a season, only Rickey Henderson has more since the 1800's, swiping 130 bags in 1982. Having led the league 8 out of the 9 seasons from 1966 to 1974, Lou would finish his career in 1979 with a total of 938 swiped bags. Combined with his .293 average and his occasional pop (149 HR), Lou was a feared and effective leadoff hitter.

Photo: Hostess (via tradingcarddb)
Illustration: Zulkifli Ramadhan Hanan

Another tiny number: Lou Brock's time to second base.

After being drafted with the 402nd pick of the 1999 draft, Albert Pujols made an immediate impact in the 2001 season, winning ROY and finishing 4th in the MVP race. He finished in the top 5 of MVP candidates in 10 of his 11 first years, winning 3 of them. Most remember him as a HR/RBI "Machine", but he currently holds .302 career BA to go along with his 632 (and counting) HR's entering the 2019 season.

Photo: Dirk Hansen (via flickr)
Illustration: Zulkifli Ramadhan Hanan

Albert's "The Machine" that launches homers at the sun.

While playing second base for the Philadelphia Athletics in 1901, Nap Lajoie led the AL in each of the 3 main hitting categories with a stat line of .426 BA / 14HR / 125 RBI, earning the rare and coveted "Triple Crown." The high average and low home run total show just how much the game has changed since that time. He would go on to win a total of 5 batting titles over his career.

Photo: Charles Conlon (via National Baseball Hall of Fame Library)
Illustration: Maruncun

Nap won the "Triple Crown" back in nineteen hundred one.

It's hard to believe that David Ortiz was once a platooning left handed hitter, struggling to find an everyday job with the Twins. The Red Sox saw potential in his swing and brought him in to hit in front of their star slugger, Manny Ramirez. This powerful 1-2 punch was a key component to the Sox 2004 & 2007 titles. Even without Manny backing him up in 2013, Ortiz would win another title after hitting .688 in the WS, also netting him that year's WS MVP.

Photo: Waldo Jaquith (via flickr)
Illustration: Zulkifli Ramadhan Hanan

Ortiz could make a pitcher's bad day even worse.

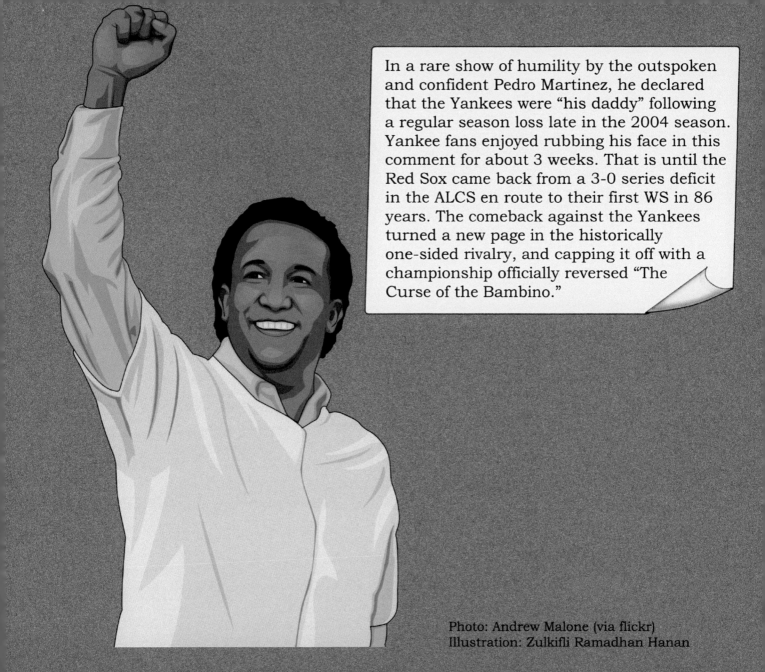

In a rare show of humility by the outspoken and confident Pedro Martinez, he declared that the Yankees were "his daddy" following a regular season loss late in the 2004 season. Yankee fans enjoyed rubbing his face in this comment for about 3 weeks. That is until the Red Sox came back from a 3-0 series deficit in the ALCS en route to their first WS in 86 years. The comeback against the Yankees turned a new page in the historically one-sided rivalry, and capping it off with a championship officially reversed "The Curse of the Bambino."

Photo: Andrew Malone (via flickr)
Illustration: Zulkifli Ramadhan Hanan

He helped his buddy *Pedro* finally "Reverse the Curse."

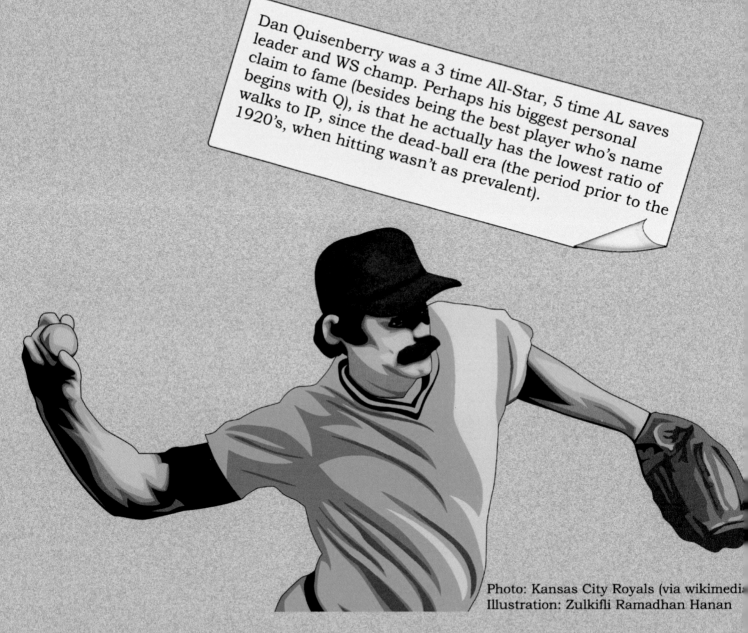

Dan Quisenberry was a 3 time All-Star, 5 time AL saves leader and WS champ. Perhaps his biggest personal claim to fame (besides being the best player who's name begins with Q), is that he actually has the lowest ratio of walks to IP, since the dead-ball era (the period prior to the 1920's, when hitting wasn't as prevalent).

Photo: Kansas City Royals (via wikimedi
Illustration: Zulkifli Ramadhan Hanan

Batters tried to get on base and go about their biz but couldn't draw a walk against Kansas City's "Quiz.

Prior to Robinson's debut for the Dodgers in 1947, black baseball players could only be seen playing in the "Negro Leagues." It took a lot of courage for Jackie to break the color barrier knowing he would face unwarranted critisism. Jackie's bravery proved to be a big stepping-stone in baseball's history and in US history as well, helping to shift the way many US citizens viewed racial segregation. On a personal level, Jackie is one of the nation's great heroes. And in strictly baseball terms, he was a hero for the Dodgers, as a WS champ, ROY, MVP, and 6 time All-Star.

Roberto Clemente was the first Latin American player to start for a WS winning team, win the NL MVP, win the WS MVP and get inducted into the HOF. With 15 All-Star appearances and 3000 hits, he was a hero on the field. Off the field, he was an even bigger hero with his charity and community service work. The "Roberto Clemente Award" is annually presented to the major league player that best demonstrates a combination of on and off the field heroics.

Photo: Bob Sandberg (via wikimedia)
Illustration: Maruncun

Photo: Jay Publishing
(via tradingcarddb)
Illustration: Maruncun

Robinson & Roberto are among the most admired. The number 42 is universally retired.

While the best player of all-time at any particular position is up for debate at most positions, Mariano Rivera stands alone as the best relief pitcher to ever take the mound. In the regular season, Mo has compiled 652 saves and a 2.21 ERA. But in 92 Postseason games, his 141 IP, 42 saves and minuscule .070 ERA helped lead the Yankees to 5 titles. Metallica's "Enter Sandman" could be aptly heard throughout Yankee Stadium whenever he took the mound. For when he'd ENTER in the NIGHT and that cutter left his hand, he liked to send his batters OFF TO NEVER-NEVER LAND.

Jersey numbers are retired by teams as a way of honoring the contributions of the players that wore them. On April 15, 1997, Jackie Robinson became the first player whose jersey number was retired not just by his own team, but by all teams, in honor of his contribution to the game as a whole. Mariano Rivera made his major league debut 2 years earlier in 1995, choosing to wear 42 to honor Jackie's legacy.

Photo: Keith Allison (via wikimedia)
Illustration: Zulkifli Ramadhan Hanan

But someone else did wear it. He grabbed it just in time. The Sandman got the call when the game was on the line.

In just his 3rd major league season, Tom Seaver helped propel the Miracle Mets to the 1969 World Series, winning the title in just their 8th year of existence. With his WS ring, ROY, no-hitter, 3 Cy Young awards, 311 Wins, and 3640 K's, he has a pretty complete resume as far as pitchers are concerned.

Photo: Shelly S (via flickr)
Illustration: Dharmawan Wicaksono

Mo upheld a standard for New York as a reliever.
As a starter, same is true of "Tom Terrific" *S*eaver.

Tom Glavine, Greg Maddux, and John Smoltz formed a trio of aces for the Braves that would alternate winning Cy Young awards throughout the 90's. Any team would have been lucky to have just one of these future HOF'ers in their rotation, but having all 3 was a main factor in Atlanta's 11 straight seasons atop the NL East from 1995-2005. Capitalizing on the craze of Mark McGuire's home run chase, Glavine & Maddux starred in a memorable commercial in which they tried to bulk up, believing that women who supposedly "dig the long ball," like Heather Locklier, would give them the type of attention that McGuire got at the time.

Photo (Tom Glavine - head):
Eric Enfermero (via wikimedia)
Photo (Greg Maddux - head):
Dirk Hansen (via wikimedia)
Photo (Weightlifter - bodies/equipment):
J Griffin (via flickr)
Illustration: Dharmawan Wicaksono

Tom Glavine dug the long ball with his training buddy Greg.

At 6'10", Randy "The Big Unit" Johnson used his long body to hurl sliders past batters, who could only swing and hope for the best. Getting batters to swing and miss helped Randy to 6 seasons of 300 strikeouts or more, a distinction he shares with Nolan Ryan. While Ryan holds the single season record during the live-ball era with 383 K's in a season, Randy had 372 in a season where he pitched 249.2 innings (compared to 326 IP in Ryan's 249.2 innings (compared to 326 IP in Ryan's record setting season).

Photo: Dirk Hansen (via flickr)
Illustration: Zulkifli Ramadhan Hanan

They and the "Big Unit"
served up many a goose egg.

No matter how far outside pitchers threw at him, Vladimir Guerrero liked to take a swing. This behavior is typically seen as a flaw for most hitters. However, Vlad's talent for making contact separated him from most hitters. Despite his penchant for reaching outside the strike zone, he struck out an average of less than 62 times per season, very low for a hitter with his power. If the first image that comes to mind when thinking of Vlad is of him lifting a ball thrown 2 inches off the plate, then the second image would be of him throwing from RF to home plate to catch a runner foolish enough to test his arm.

Photo: Keith Allison (via wikimedia)
Illustration: Zulkifli Ramadhan Hanan

Vlad excelled from both ends
hitting bombs and making plays.

Photo: Jay Publishing (via tradingcarddb)
Illustration: Zulkifli Ramadhan Hanan

I wonder if his arm could catch
the speedy Willie Mays.

Jimmie Foxx was the epitome of consistency, with 12 consecutive seasons with at least 30 HR, 13 straight with over 100 RBI, and a career .325 average. In 1933, one of his 3 MVP seasons, he won the Triple Crown with a line of .356 BA / 48 HR / 163 RBI.

Photo: Harris & Ewing (via LOC)
Illustration: Zulkifli Ramadhan Hanan

With Jimmie "Double X"
pitchers struggled to relax.

Leading either the AL or the NL in all 3 of the main pitching categories (Wins, ERA, and Strikeouts) earns a pitcher the Triple Crown. It's happened 38 times in the history of baseball. 3 of those belong to Sandy Koufax. Grover Cleveland Alexander and Walter Johnson are the only other pitchers who have achieved this 3 times. Although Sandy's Triple Crowns didn't just lead his own league (NL), but both leagues, which sets his apart from many others. Oh, and he's also got 4 WS rings & 4 no-hitters, 1 of which is a perfect game.

Photo: University of Southern California Libraries & California Historical Society
Illustration: Moch. Suyuti Amien

Unless they threw a curve like that of pitching great, Koufa X.

He earned more rings (13) than he had fingers (10) to put them on. He graced the world with more "Yogi-isms" (countless) than he had All-Star appearances (18). Lastly, Yogi Berra won his 3 MVP awards with gameplay that was 90% mental; the other half was physical.

Photo: Bowman Gum (via wikimedia)
Illustration: Suyudi Indrawijaya

"It ain't over til it's over," said catcher, Yogi Berra.

Ozzie Smith has career totals of 8,375 assists (2nd only to Rabbit Maranville), and 1,590 double plays (2nd only to Omar Vizquel). Turning all those double plays earned him 13 consecutive Gold Gloves at Shortstop from 1980-1992. A legend in the infield as a defender, he was also quite comfortable on the base paths as a runner, with 580 stolen bases.

Photo (head): Johnmaxmena
(via wikimedia)
Photo (body): Family Fun Centers
(via tradingcarddb)
Illustration: Moch. Suyuti Amien

Which brings us down to OZZie - the best fielder of his era.

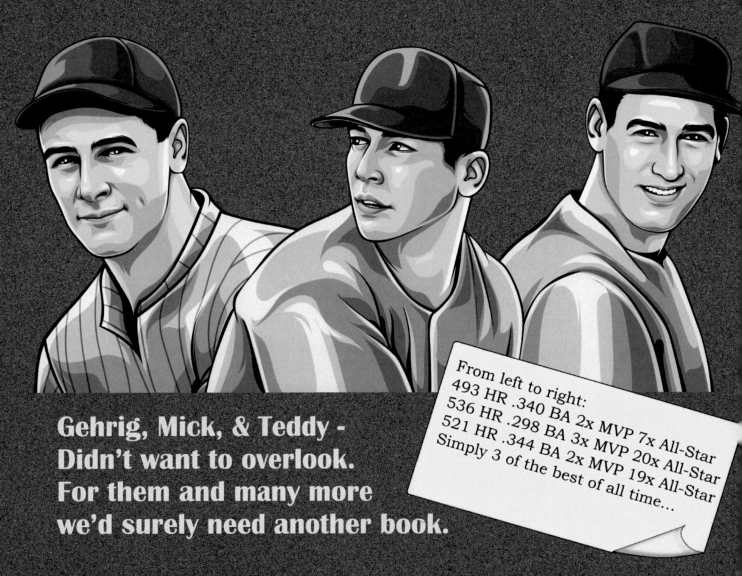

Photo (Lou Gehrig): Pacific & Atlantic Photos, Inc (via wikimedia)
Photo (Mickey Mantle): Jay Publishing (via milehighcardco)
Photo (Ted Williams): Jay Publishing (via psacard)
Illustrations: Dharmawan Wicaksono

Gehrig, Mick, & Teddy -
Didn't want to overlook.
For them and many more
we'd surely need another book.

From left to right:
493 HR .340 BA 2x MVP 7x All-Star
536 HR .298 BA 3x MVP 20x All-Star
521 HR .344 BA 2x MVP 19x All-Star
Simply 3 of the best of all time...

Well now we're at the end, so without further ado
let's sing our ABC's from the top all the way through.

ABCDEFG HIJKLMNOP QRS TUV WX YZ

Now you know more legends of the game.
Hope you saw your favorite's name.
If you didn't, that's a shame.
Hope you'll find him at the "Hall of Fame".

We just used our ABC's
to name the Best of the Best of the Major Leagues.

Photo: Map data ©2018 Google
Illustration: Danijel Vujanović

Career Batting Statistics

Player	Years Active	R	HR	RBI	SB	BA	Teams
Hank Aaron	1954-76	2174	755	2297	240	.305	ATL MIL
Babe Ruth	1914-35	2174	714	2214	123	.342	NYY BOS BSN
Joe DiMaggio	1936-42, '46-51	1390	361	1537	30	.325	NYY
Ernie Banks	1953-71	1305	512	1636	50	.274	CHC
Frank Thomas	1990-08	1494	521	1704	32	.301	CHW OAK TOR
Ken Griffey Jr.	1989-10	1662	630	1836	184	.284	SEA CIN CHW
Honus Wagner	1897-17	1739	101	1732	723	.328	PIT LOU
Ichiro Suzuki	2001-18*	1420	117	780	509	.311	SEA NYY MIA
Derek Jeter	1995-14	1923	260	1311	358	.310	NYY
Lou Brock	1961-79	1610	149	900	938	.293	STL CHC
Albert Pujols	2001-18*	1773	633	1982	111	.302	STL LAA
Nap Lajoie	1896-16	1504	82	1599	380	.338	CLE PHI PHA
David Ortiz	1997-16	1419	541	1768	17	.286	BOS MIN
Jackie Robinson	1947-56	947	137	734	197	.311	BRO
Roberto Clemente	1955-72	1416	240	1305	83	.317	PIT
Vladimir Guerrero	1996-11	1328	449	1496	181	.318	MON LAA TEX BAL
Willie Mays	1951-73	2062	660	1903	338	.302	SFG NYM
Jimmie Foxx	1925-45	1751	534	1922	87	.325	PHA BOS CHC PHI
Yogi Berra	1946-63 65	1175	358	1430	30	.285	NYY NYM
Ozzie Smith	1978-96	1257	28	793	580	.262	STL SDP
Lou Gehrig	1923-39	1888	493	1995	102	.340	NYY
Mickey Mantle	1951-68	1676	536	1509	153	.298	NYY
Ted Williams	1939-42, '46-60	1798	521	1839	24	.344	BOS

*Active Players Stats through 2018

Career Pitching Statistics

Player	Years Active	W-L	SV	IP	ERA	K	Teams
Babe Ruth	1914-35	94-46	4	1221.1	2.28	488	NYY BOS BSN
Cy Young	1890-11	511-315	18	7356	2.63	2803	CLV BOS CLE STL BSN
Clayton Kershaw	2008-18*	153-69	0	2096.1	2.39	2275	LAD
Pedro Martinez	1992-09	219-100	3	2827.1	2.93	3154	BOS NYM MON LAD PHI
Dan Quisenberry	1979-90	56-46	244	1043.1	2.76	379	KCR STL SFG
Mariano Rivera	1995-13	82-60	652	1283.2	2.21	1173	NYY
Tom Seaver	1967-86	311-205	1	4783	2.86	3640	NYM CIN CHW BOS
Greg Maddux	1986-08	355-227	0	5008.1	3.16	3371	ATL CHC LAD SDP
Tom Glavine	1987-08	305-203	0	4413.1	3.54	2607	ATL NYM
Randy Johnson	1988-09	303-166	2	4135.1	3.29	4875	SEA ARI MON NYY SFG HOU
Sandy Koufax	1955-66	165-87	9	2324.1	2.76	2396	BRO LAD

*Active Players Stats through 2018

Acronyms and Definitions

Professional Baseball Leagues	
MLB	Major League Baseball - The predominant professional baseball league in the US & Canada
AL	American League - 1 of 2 Leagues in the MLB (the one with the DH)
NL	National League - 1 of 2 Leagues in the MLB (the one where pitchers bat)
NPB	Nippon Professional Baseball - The predominant professional baseball league in Japan (where Ichiro played)

Distinctions/Awards	
GG	Gold Glove Award - Awarded to the best fielding player at a position in the AL or NL
AS	All-Star - A player that's earned the oppurtunity to represent the AL or NL in the midseason All-Star game
Cy Young	An award for the pitcher with best regular season performance in either the AL or NL
MVP	Most Valuable Player - Awarded to the player with the best overall performance the regular season for the AL or NL
WS MVP	World Series MVP - Awarded to the player with the best overall performance in the World Series
Triple Crown	A pitcher that leads either the AL or NL in all 3 of these categories: W, ERA, K
Triple Crown	A batter that leads either the AL or NL in all 3 of these categories: HR, RBI, BA

Other Terms Used	
WS	World Series - The championship of the MLB where the AL champ faces the NL champ in a best of seven game series
#RE2PECT	A play on the word Respect and Jeter's jersey number, an ad campaign by Nike, and a social media hashtag
Goose Egg	A metaphor for the shape of a 0, as in a pitcher holding the opposing team to 0 runs in an IP or game

Statistics

Batting		Pitching	
R	Runs	W	Wins
HR	Home Runs	L	Losses
RBI	Runs Batted In	SV	Saves
SB	Stolen Bases	IP	Inning Pitched
BA	Batting Average	ERA	Earned Run Average
		K	Strikeouts

Positions

P	Pitcher	3B	Third Base
SP	Starting Pitcher	SS	Short Stop
RP	Relief Pitcher	RF	Right Field
C	Catcher	CF	Center Field
1B	First Base	LF	Left Field
2B	Second Base	DH	Designated Hitter

Team Abbreviations

American League					
EAST		CENTRAL		WEST	
BAL	Baltimore Orioles	CLE	Cleveland Indians	HOU	Houston Astros
BOS	Boston Red Sox	CHW	Chicago White Sox	LAA	Los Angeles Angels of Anaheim
NYY	New York Yankees	DET	Detroit Tigers	OAK	Oakland Athletics
TBR	Tampa Bay Rays	KCR	Kansas City Royals	SEA	Seattle Mariners
TOR	Toronto Blue Jays	MIN	Minnesota Twins	TEX	Texas Rangers

National League					
EAST		CENTRAL		WEST	
ATL	Atlanta Braves	CHC	Chicago Cubs	ARI	Arizona Diamondbacks
PHI	Philadelphia Phillies	CIN	Cincinnati Reds	COL	Colorado Rockies
MIA	Miami Marlins	MIL	Milwaukee Brewers	LAD	Los Angeles Dodgers
NYM	New York Mets	PIT	Pittsburgh Pirates	SDP	San Diego Padres
WSN	Washington Nationals	STL	St. Louis Cardinals	SFG	San Fransisco Giants

Defunct Teams Referenced	
BSN	Boston Braves
BRO	Brooklyn Dodgers
CLV	Cleveland Spiders
MON	Montreal Expos
LOU	Louisville Colonels
PHA	Philadelphia Athletics

For a complete list of all team abbreviations throughout history check out:

https://www.baseball-reference.com/about/team_IDs.shtml

Thank You for reading!

ISBN: 978-1-091-21382-1
Text protected by copyright © Owl Eye Books, Inc - 2019

The athletes portrayed in this book were not contacted by Owl Eye Books, Inc. regarding their inclusion. Therefore, their inclusions in the book do not constitute an endorsement of any kind. Rather, their factual portrayals should be considered "expressive use" for editorial and educational purposes.

All of the illustrations were based off actual photographs taken of each player or building. Use of every photograph is permissible by virtue of either being part of the public domain or being covered under a "Creative Commons" copyright. Attribution for each photo is underneath each illustration.

Visit the website below for a complete list of all of the sources for all photographs that were illustrated in this book:

https://www.owleyebooks.com/legends-of-baseball-from-aa-to-zz

Photographs licensed under a Creative Commons "Share Alike" license mandate "If you remix, transform, or build upon the material, you must distribute your contributions under the same license as the original." Therefore, the seven photographs licensed under a "Share Alike" license are redistributed under the same terms in the flickr album below:

https://flic.kr/s/aHsmGQBb7d

We love hearing from and interacting with our readers.
Please feel free to:

   Follow Us!
@OwlEyeBooks

 Visit Us!
https://OwlEyeBooks.com

 E-mail Us!
OwlEyeBooks@gmail.com

OWL EYE BOOKS

https://www.owleyebooks.com

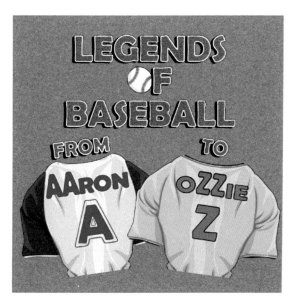

Made in the USA
Monee, IL
08 January 2020

20069627R00024